Liz Curtis Higgs

Loved by God

Trusting His Promises & Experiencing His Blessings

Leader Guide

SAMPSON RESOURCES
4887 Alpha, Suite 220 • Dallas, Texas 75244
(972) 387-2806 • (800) 371-5248 • FAX 972-387-0150
WWW.SAMPSONRESOURCES.COM   INFO@SAMPSONRESOURCES.COM

© 2004 THE SAMPSON COMPANY (ALL RIGHTS RESERVED)

Copyright ©2004 Liz Curtis Higgs

All Scripture quotations are taken from the *Holy Bible, New International Version*®. NIV®. Copyright © 1973, 1978, 1984 by the International Bible Society. Used by permission of Zondervan Publishing House. All rights reserved.

All rights reserved. Reproduction or duplication in any form of all or any portion of the material contained in this publication is strictly prohibited by U.S. copyright law.

What others are saying about Liz Curtis Higgs and *Loved by God*

"*Loved by God* is a must for every women's ministry!"
Debbie Stuart, Director of Women's Ministry
Prestonwood Baptist Church, Dallas, TX

"What a master storyteller Liz is. She makes the Bible come alive."
Amie Price, Women's Ministries
RiverTree Christian Church, Massillon, OH

"*Loved by God* is an inspiring Bible study. You'll be blessed. And I love the workbook!"
Melissa Shaver, Director of Women's Ministries
The Heights Baptist Church, Richardson, TX

"I am constantly amazed at Liz's biblical depth, understanding, and the tremendous way she shares it. Truly, she has been anointed of God."
Evelyn Blount, Executive Director
South Carolina Women's Missionary Union

"*Loved by God* will touch your heart and encourage your spirit."
Kay Daigle, Women's Ministry Director
Northwest Bible Church, Dallas, TX

"Liz was a hit with our audience! She is a gift to my life!"
Gloria Gaither, Praise Gathering, Indianapolis, IN

"We have laughed and cried and been encouraged that God loves us."
Debra Lavin, President, Alliance Women
First Alliance Church, Erie, PA

"Liz is a true master at touching the hearts of people. She's fantastic!"
Judy Russell, wife of Bob Russell, Senior Minister
Southeast Christian Church, Louisville, KY

CONTENTS

SECTION I — PREPARING FOR THE STUDY

A Note from Liz Curtis Higgs 4

A Four-Part Bible Study 5

Suggested Meeting Formats 6

Planning and Promotion 7

Leadership Guidelines 8

Twelve Tips for Small Group Leaders 9

Eight Simple Ways to Encourage Women to Study the Bible 10

Prayer Recommendations 11

Weekly Session Format 12

SECTION II — LEADING THE STUDY

Introduction **WELCOME TO THE FAMILY!** 14
God's Plans for Us Are Bigger Than We Can Imagine

Week 1 **SIBLING RIVALRY** 15
God Honors His Promises, Even When We Don't

Week 2 **RUNNING FROM GOD** 17
God Knows All About Prodigal Children

Week 3 **A DREAM COME TRUE** 20
God's Love Knows No Bounds

Week 4 **BLINDED BY LOVE** 23
Man Looks at the Outward Appearance;
God Looks at the Heart

Week 5 **A DECEIVER DECEIVED** 26
God Disciplines the Ones He Loves

Week 6 **A HEART FOR GOD** 29
God's Love Is Powerful Enough to Change Our Hearts

A Note from Liz Curtis Higgs

elcome to *Loved by God,* a six-week, in-depth Bible study designed especially for my sisters in Christ! Together, you and I will help women learn how to embrace God's unconditional love, trust God's wonderful promises, and accept God's countless blessings, even on those days when we feel we don't deserve them.

God gave us his holy Word—the Bible—to teach us who he is and how we are to respond to him. Your heartfelt commitment to lead this study is a big step, but have no fear—you are *not* alone. Just as others will be praying for you, I will carry you in my heart as well, grateful to have you partnering with me in this unique learning opportunity. I know God will use you to touch the lives of women by leading them, praying for them, and learning with them.

As I wrote this study, thinking about the women who will walk through your door, I kept three goals in mind: that they will discover how much God loves them; that they will realize they can trust God's promises; and that they will experience God's blessings in an eye-opening, life-changing way. Anything you can do to help accomplish these goals will serve your women well.

This Leader Guide has been created to help you plan, promote, and direct the study of *Loved by God.* On the following pages you will find detailed information on the four parts of this Bible study, suggested meeting formats, thoughts on planning and promotion, leadership guidelines, tips for small group leaders, simple ways to encourage women to study God's Word, and prayer recommendations. May God guide you through the weeks to come!

LEADER GUIDE

A Four-Part Bible Study

There are four elements to this Bible study: personal study, group discussion, principles and applications, and video sessions. All parts are equally important. Let's look at them.

Personal Study: The purpose of the workbook is to give participants an organized way to spend time with God daily as they read the Scriptures and answer the questions for that day. Encourage the women to find a specific time each day for study and to follow the five-day schedule. This plan will help them absorb the material in small increments rather than being overwhelmed at the end of the week. It also helps participants reflect throughout the week on what they're learning. Many women may be participating in a Bible study for the first time. Assure them of the value of a disciplined study time, and recommend that they answer the questions themselves, using the Bible as their primary source, rather than ask others for their opinions. This way the answers are more personal, more scriptural, and therefore more meaningful. Even if a woman is stumped by a question, she can look forward to the group discussion time when she'll hear others' perspectives and no doubt discover she isn't the only one who struggles at times to answer a question.

Group Discussion: The group discussion period will be a vital weekly feature of the study. Depending on the number of participants, this may require dividing into several smaller groups. It is suggested that there be no more than twelve in a group. Women will be encouraged to share their workbook answers from their daily study time, creating a sense of Christian fellowship, bonding, and accountability within the group. They'll look forward to hearing one another's responses to specific questions, which will help give them perspective on the subject as well as enhance their understanding of Scripture.

Principles and Applications: For Bible study to become a heart-changing, life-transforming experience, we must *identify* the principles at work and *apply* them to our personal situations. Therefore, a key part of each week's class is a time to discuss principles and applications so that women are encouraged to move from *studying* God's Word to *applying* it daily.

Principles are timeless truths found in Scripture—simple, straightforward truths that can be applied to our lives today. Some of the women in your group may be new at studying God's Word, so you will need to guide them through this process. Encourage women not to *read into* the Scriptures but instead to *pull out* truth from the verses they are studying.

Application means putting into practice the principles found in Scripture. When we help women move forward from principles to application, the value of Bible study increases exponentially.

To help women transition from ancient story to modern lifestyle, you will find in this Leader Guide one principle and one application that can be drawn from each lesson. Encourage the class to discuss other possible principles and applications they gleaned from the study, and share your own insights as well. People will suggest different applications because of their unique circumstances, which will expand the group's awareness of God's relevance in our daily lives.

Some of your attendees will have studied God's Word for many years and will move through principles and applications quickly. For those women, your challenge will be to teach them to discover fresh truths in familiar material. Urge them to look for new applications. Since these women may be at different stages in their lives since the last time they studied this story, they will have new eyes to see old truths. As you lead them through this part of the discussion, you may want to

frequently remind them to apply these truths to experiences that have occurred in the last few months. We don't want to live in the past; rather, we want to apply Scripture in ever-new ways that address our current circumstances.

Video Sessions: Each session on DVD is thirty minutes long. The women will gain new insights as they listen to the weekly teaching from Genesis, covered verse by verse—a teaching enhanced by extensive biblical research and personal experience. The women will participate during the video session through careful listening, by taking notes in the space allotted in their workbooks, and also by laughing. All three methods—listening, note taking, and laughing—contribute to the learning process. Hearing the Scripture presented in this way will help women remember the verses they've studied as well as the lessons they've learned.

Suggested Meeting Formats

Loved by God is a flexible Bible study for women, suitable for various time frames and environments. Three possible meeting formats follow that allow for different settings—church, classroom, or home—and one to two hours designated for the study. Some women enjoy a time of fellowship with snacks and drinks before the meeting begins. Others who are concerned with busy schedules may prefer to get directly into the study. Pray about the format that best suits the women who will be involved.

Whatever schedule you follow, allow time for the women to move from one element to the next—opening, discussion, video—and keep announcements and distractions to a minimum.

If childcare is offered, be sure to schedule drop-off *prior* to the official starting time for the Bible study. Regardless, make sure the women understand that class will begin promptly at the time designated...then start on time!

One-Hour Bible Study Format

10 minutes: **Group Participation**—Have prayer requests written out by participants in advance so requests can be handled succinctly.
15 minutes: **Discussion Time**—Review only the questions that require explanation or have strong, biblical concepts that need to be emphasized. Discuss at least one principle from the week and its possible applications. Encourage the women to make notes in the "After Your Group Discussion…" box in their workbooks.
30 minutes: **Video**—Watch the video together.
5 minutes: **Closing Prayer/Encouragement for the Week**—Send them off with a prayer and a promise of what is to come.

Ninety-Minute Bible Study Format (recommended)

10 minutes: **Large Group Participation**—Welcome everyone and open with a prayer. Consider spending a short time in worship to prepare hearts.
30 minutes: **Small Group Discussion**—Review the workbook questions and discuss the primary principles and applications from the week's lessons. Allow a few minutes at the end of this time for participants to fill in the "After Your Group Discussion…" boxes.
10 minutes: **Small Group Prayer Time**—Spend a few minutes praying for each other's needs.
30 minutes: **Video**—Gather everyone to watch the video.

10 minutes: **Closing Prayer/Encouragement for the Week**—Bring a sense of closure to the class time and give a brief preview of the next lesson. Include points from the video in your prayer. Encourage them to do their personal study daily.

Two-Hour Bible Study Format

10 minutes:	**Fellowship/Refreshments**
10 minutes:	**Large Group Participation**
40 minutes:	**Small Group Discussion**
15 minutes:	**Small Group Prayer Time**
5 minutes:	**Short Break**
30 minutes:	**Video**
10 minutes:	**Closing Prayer/Encouragement for the Week**

Planning and Promotion

Once you have chosen the day, time, and format for the seven weeks of your Bible study, detailed preparation can begin. Here are some important points to consider:

♦ **Budget**—Meet with a staff representative and learn the goals of the church regarding this study as a resource to area women. If the church sees this as an outreach ministry and has sufficient funds in the budget, you may want to provide workbooks at no cost or set up a supplemental fund to reduce the price of the workbooks for participants.

♦ **Room Reservation**—If you have chosen to meet at the church building, work with the facilities coordinator to have a room reserved on a weekly basis for the event. Agree on the room layout so that it looks the same each week. The arrangement of tables and chairs depends on the size of your study. Here are two suggestions for room setup: (1) Place round tables with eight chairs each throughout the room. Every table represents a small group. Have the women sit at their designated table each week. This can become their place for small group discussion as well as prayer time. The women can turn their chairs for viewing the video. (2) Organize the space in classroom style with rectangular tables and chairs. The women can sit at the tables for the opening and then move their chairs into smaller circles for the discussion period. Or they can all be together for discussion time and move to smaller, intimate circles for prayer time.

♦ **Childcare coordination**—If childcare will be offered, you'll need to work with your preschool minister or the person responsible for that department to schedule babysitters and to ensure that all insurance concerns are addressed. If you will be meeting in a private home, you may want to arrange for an older teenager to watch the children. Or schedule rotations of two women each week to watch the children during the discussion and video times.

♦ **Promotion**—Good promotion is necessary for a successful Bible study. Women won't know about this exciting opportunity unless you tell them! Place posters around the church describing the study, time, location, price, and childcare registration information. The kit includes various promotional items for use in your church bulletin or newsletter. In addition, the graphics files and promotional copy are included on audio CD #4 in a folder/directory for use on your computer. Simply insert the CD into the CD drive of your computer and open the directory of the CD. A folder/directory will appear on the screen with promotional materials inside, which you can copy and paste into your own documents.

- **Registration**—Set up a table at a convenient spot for women to register after they attend church services or Bible classes. Have leaders available to answer questions about the study. Early registration is important so you can evaluate the needs of your group, determine how many small group leaders will be needed, create those small groups, and pray for those who have registered. Small group dynamics work best with eight to twelve women per group. On your registration list, request all the information you might need: name, age, occupation, telephone number, e-mail address, and childcare needs. This will allow you to prepare in advance for group size and childcare requirements.
- **Nametags**—People enjoy knowing the name of those they meet! Prepare nametags in advance for those who have registered. A JPEG file is included on the promotional CD (audio CD #4) that you can use in your word processor to create your own nametags, or you can use prepackaged nametags if you prefer. Have temporary blank nametags at the first session for women who come without having registered in advance. Make sure everyone feels welcome!
- **TV/DVD equipment**—Reserve all equipment needed for the seven weeks (Introduction plus six weeks of study), and make certain the equipment is set up and working an hour or more before the meeting starts.

Leadership Guidelines

Depending on the size of the Bible study group and the location of your weekly meetings, various leaders will be needed to make the study successful and enjoyable for everyone. If you have a group of sixteen women or more, you will need to form small groups for discussion. This will create an intimate setting, allow more women to share their workbook answers, and be less intimidating for the quieter participants. For the sake of this guide, we will assume the numbers are higher than sixteen women. Feel free to adjust the following guidelines based on the needs of your group.

Director—She is the liaison to the church staff and should be strong in all aspects of leadership. She has the gift of administration and is good at making decisions on the spot and resolving problems. She may have led Bible studies in the past and already be familiar with the many details that must be managed. She is prepared to motivate her team and works well with different personalities, helping everyone accept and enjoy each other. The director will need to prayerfully consider and recruit the rest of the leaders long before the introductory session. Prayer is essential in that process. Even though a person is gifted as a leader, she might be going through a stressful time and not be ready to lead others at the moment. Remember, the director and the small group leaders don't need to be Bible teachers, but they do need to be good facilitators.

Small Group Leader—This person is strong in her faith, growing in her relationship with the Lord, and nurturing and compassionate to other women. She has a heart for encouraging women to grow in Christ. A good small group leader prays for her women daily, prepares her questions in advance, and prayerfully considers which questions will be best to discuss each session. She has the ability to move the women smoothly from question to question and makes everyone feel comfortable, whether they are new to the Bible or have studied God's Word for years. A skilled small group leader will manage the process so that everyone participates, including the quieter ones. An effective small group leader is willing to contact people individually and prays with them when a need arises.

Secretary—This detail-oriented woman ensures the workbooks have been ordered and made available and takes care of the introductory meeting particulars: nametags, workbook sales, and getting the A-V equipment in place and working. She may want to keep an updated list of attendees. She may also call or e-mail women each week to encourage them.

Refreshment/Fellowship Coordinator—This person loves any social event! She coordinates the weekly refreshments with the women. If a closing celebration dinner or fellowship time before or after the final session is planned, she will coordinate everything for that event.

Twelve Tips for Small Group Leaders

1. To capture everyone's attention from the very start, consider using a visual aid, a meaningful poem, a surprising statistic, a relevant news story, a pithy question, or anything else that will illustrate the Genesis narrative and engage the women's interest. You'll also find here a suggested Welcome Warmup for each week's lesson. Feel free to be creative and come up with something else that suits your own style and your group's needs.

2. Small groups quickly develop a "prayer personality": chattier groups like to pray for the needs of individuals who are present, while studious groups prefer sticking to a brief prayer for the session and plunging into the workbook questions. You will set the tone for the weeks to follow. Consider carefully how much time you want to allow each week for prayer and how comfortable your group will be with sharing such needs. Short and to the point is the best way to begin; otherwise this sharing time can easily take over the study time!

3. Relax in knowing that your primary role is to facilitate the discussion of what the women have learned in their private Bible study time the previous week. You don't need to have the answers to all the questions that might arise. Your job is to keep things on track, biblically and practically, and to make your group session upbeat and productive for everyone.

4. Good listening skills—smiling, nodding, maintaining eye contact—communicate to each woman that her words matter and her involvement is appreciated. Such validation is one of the most important things a facilitator can do. Call each group member by name and make her feel welcome with everything you say and do.

5. Create a nonthreatening atmosphere for discussion. Instead of correcting or criticizing—even nonverbally with a wrinkled brow or slight frown—focus on helping women find the most biblically sound answers to their questions. Keep things positive. Say "Yes, and…" rather than "No, but…" If someone gets long-winded, gently summarize her comments and move on. If someone rambles or seems confused, clarify her comments as best you can and get back on track. In either case, thank her for contributing.

6. Encourage the quieter class members to participate without putting them on the spot. If they are looking at you, they are probably prepared to share. If they have their heads down or their eyes averted, wait for another question. Try to balance the participation so that a few people don't dominate the discussion each week. Your more reticent members will appreciate it.

7. Keep the discussion directed toward the Bible and personal application so comments don't stray into nonproductive speculation. Human opinions are interesting, but biblical truth is *life changing!* After all, the goal of Bible study is to learn more about the Bible, not more about each other, delightful as that is. Keeping God's Word at the center of your discussion time will bear much fruit.

8. Please review the video lesson on DVD or CD each week *before* your group meets. That way you can steer your class discussion away from material you know will be covered, avoiding redundancy. Plus you can prepare their hearts for the message to follow.

9. Resist the temptation to do most of the talking. Rather than sharing what *you* have discovered, urge others to share what *they* have discovered. Offer your comments after other women have offered theirs and only if your answer enhances, rather than repeats, what has already been said. This takes discipline…but you can do it, sis!

10. Encourage participants to raise questions that came up during the week. If you don't have the answer, promise to do further study and come back the next week with additional insights. One of the real joys of facilitating is gleaning new truths about God's Word from solid commentaries and research books and from people who are farther along in their spiritual growth.

11. Engender enthusiasm for the next week's lesson with a "teaser" about what's to come. You'll find a bit of that at the end of each video. See if you, too, can find something in the next lesson that will pique the women's interest and keep them coming back.

12. Check out one or more of the fifteen resources suggested at the end of the workbook to further your understanding of the passages in this Bible study. The ones listed are a good starting point, but many excellent commentaries are available, especially on the book of Genesis. If your church doesn't have a library, your pastor might let you peruse his study shelves. Or visit your local Christian bookstore and make some good investments in your own spiritual growth.

Eight Simple Ways to Encourage Women to Study the Bible

Our hearts' desire is to see women's lives changed by the timeless truths of Scripture. Here are some easy points to share—in your own words if you prefer—to convince your attendees that daily Bible study is truly worth the time and effort.

1. *You can handle it!* This study centers on a relatively small portion of Scripture, so each day's Bible study can be done in twenty to thirty minutes.

2. *Take it easy on yourself!* Do one lesson each day rather than doing all five days at once. That way God Word's can penetrate your heart and be reinforced daily.

3. *Love those stories!* We're studying a portion of Scripture that is entirely narrative, and don't we all enjoy a good story? Even those of us who think we know this tale will come to see these people and events in a new way.

4. *You're not alone!* When you study the Bible, you're in good company. The Holy Spirit moves in your heart, teaching you, guiding you, and empowering you.

5. *Make it special!* Select a pleasant spot to study each day, a place as free from distraction as possible. Let your family know this is *your* time with God.

6. *Write it on your heart!* Memorize key verses or write them out and place them in a prominent place as a way to instill God's principles in your heart and mind.

7. *Check it out!* In addition to using your favorite Bible, check out other translations as well. Web sites can change quickly, but http://bible.gospelcom.net is a good one, providing access to at least seventeen versions, including the New International Version, the New American Standard Bible, the Amplified Bible, the New King James Version, and more contemporary Bibles such as The Message and the New Living Translation.

8. *Give God room!* Remember that God's Word is "living and active. Sharper than any double-edged sword, it penetrates even to dividing soul and spirit, joints and marrow; it judges the thoughts and attitudes of the heart" (Hebrews 4:12). If you want to grow, you have to give God access to your heart and let his Word do its mighty work.

Prayer Recommendations

Prayer is by far the most important part of any Bible study. As soon as you decide to lead this study, begin to pray for every aspect, including the promotion, the registration, the technical details, even the atmosphere of the weekly meetings. Above all, pray for women's hearts to be open to learning more about God and applying his truth to their lives as they begin to grow in his wisdom.

If you are a director, pray for your leaders, specifically that they will guide their women toward God's truth and that there will be no complications during the weekly study times. Pray that God will use you to encourage your leaders and to teach them new ways to help others.

If you are a small group leader, pray for the women in your group and let them know you pray for them regularly. Pray that the women will bond as a group and discover they can depend on each other. Pray for the time in your small group to go smoothly. Pray that hard-to-understand questions will be answered in a way that brings contentment, not contention. Pray for discernment in knowing which questions to review each week and which principles and applications will be the most effective. For any questions that might require additional explanation, pray that you will address each one without fear or concern. God is the Leader of your group. Trust him to guide you.

Weekly Session Format

Your Bible study may involve hundreds of women and dozens of small groups, or it may be a circle of friends sitting around a living room. It may be confined to one hour or extend to two hours or more. Whatever your style or circumstances, here is a detailed checklist you might want to follow each week.

Preparation

- Pray for each woman throughout the week.
- Have the Welcome Warmup copied onto cards or slips of paper for the women to receive as they come in.
- Touch base with the members of your team (church administrator, small group leaders, secretary, refreshment coordinator) by telephone, e-mail, or a face-to-face meeting to make sure their responsibilities have been fulfilled and they are ready for the Bible study.
- Make certain the tables, chairs, and equipment will be available and set up in advance.
- Arrive early to prepare yourself and pray for the week's study.

Opening

- Have the women pick up the Welcome Warmup card as they come in, and encourage them to take a moment to read the card and prepare their thoughts as the rest of the class arrives.
- Welcome everyone and open with a prayer.
- Consider spending a short time in worship to help women turn their hearts toward God.

Welcome Warmup

- Open the discussion time with the Welcome Warmup exercise or some other activity you have created to lead into the week's lessons.

Group Discussion

- Determine in advance which questions from the week's lesson are the *most* critical to cover in the discussion period, and make sure to address those. Generally these will not be questions involving the basics of the biblical story, which are thoroughly covered in the video. Instead choose those questions that were more difficult to answer or required more personal introspection. Encourage the women to answer *all* the questions during the week, even though not all will be covered in your group time.
- After you've discussed your selected questions, ask the group for any other questions they'd like to cover before moving on to principles and application.
- As you have opportunity, reinforce the three goals mentioned in the introductory video:
  1. To know how much God loves us
  2. To realize we can trust his promises—as long as we don't insist God meet our timetables
  3. To experience God's blessings—as long as we are willing to look at a new definition of "blessing"

Principle and Application

- The Leader Guide outlines the steps for each week's lesson and suggests a principle and application for each day of the study. After prayerful consideration, select one or two principles from the week, as well as the corresponding applications, to share and discuss with your group.
- Taking this next step—applying the truths of God's Word to our lives—truly opens eyes and hearts, encouraging women to move up another level in their study time with God.
- Encourage the class to discuss other principles and applications they may have gleaned from the study, and share your own insights as well.
- Allow a few minutes at the end of this time for participants to fill in the "After Your Group Discussion…" boxes in their workbooks before starting the video.

Video

- Encourage the women as they watch to jot down in their Video Notes section the points that are especially meaningful to them. You may want to make your notes when you preview the video.
- Gather and watch the video as a group.

Closing Prayer/Encouragement for the Week

- Briefly share your favorite point from the video to encourage the women as you bring the class to a close for the week.
- Assure them that your time together has been a blessing for you and that you hope they've gained from it as well.
- Let them know what they will be studying in the week ahead.
- Close the meeting with a prayer. You may want to use something from the video as a prayer focus.

Now that you have a description of the weekly elements, in the following pages you'll find specific guidelines for each of the seven weeks, including the daily principles and applications. May God bless you richly as you lead women toward an amazing truth: they are *loved by God!*

Loved by God

INTRODUCTION

Welcome to the Family!

God's Plans for Us Are Bigger Than We Can Imagine

Scriptures for the week:
Genesis 25:19-28

OPENING

- Welcome the women.
- Introduce yourself and tell them of your excitement and anticipation for the Bible study.
- There are many clever ways to begin bonding the women. Come up with a brief icebreaker that will liven the room with laughter.
- Allow the women to introduce themselves and quickly tell something about their lives (maybe who lives in their home, how long they've lived in the area, or their favorite pastime). Whatever the size of your group, keep this time short.
- Introduce other leaders for the Bible study.

EXPECTATIONS OF THE BIBLE STUDY

- Describe the four parts of the study.
- Outline the format for the study and how each weekly session will flow. Make sure participants understand that you will begin on time each week.
- Explain the Welcome Warmup.
- Encourage everyone to complete the workbook questions each week so the discussion time will be meaningful and productive.
- Assure them that their personal study time will take no more than twenty to thirty minutes each day. Of course, the more they put into the study, the more they will be blessed!

VIDEO

- Watch the video as a group.

CLOSING PRAYER/ENCOURAGEMENT FOR THE WEEK

- Tell them that over the next week they'll be studying the actions and motives of some well-known characters from the Old Testament. They will soon see that, despite our behavior, God honors his promises.

LEADER GUIDE

WEEK ONE

Sibling Rivalry

God Honors His Promises, Even When We Don't

Scriptures for the week:
Genesis 25:27-34;
26:34-35; 27:1-29

CHECKLIST

❏ Preparation completed
❏ Welcome Warmups copied

WELCOME WARMUP

As the women come in, give them this statement printed on a card: *Share a time when you didn't receive the discipline you deserved; instead, you received mercy from another individual.*

OPENING

Begin on time. Welcome the women and open in prayer. As you pray, include elements in the prayer that will bring to mind the past week's lesson as well as point ahead to the principles and applications that will be discussed later in the session. This will help women leave behind any outside distractions and prepare their hearts to focus on the Bible study and the lessons God has for them.

GROUP DISCUSSION

→ **Warmup:** Ask the members of your group to share a time in which they didn't receive the discipline they deserved but were the recipients of someone's mercy instead. (If necessary, share an example from your own life to get the discussion started.)

After listening to the women's comments, remind everyone to incorporate what they've learned about undeserved mercy into their discussion of the week's questions by making this point: *Grace is a gift, not a reward for good behavior. Mercy is extended* because *of God's divine nature and faithfulness and* despite *our human nature and lack of faithfulness.*

Discussion: Have attendees open to their prepared answers for this week's lesson. Cover the most important questions. Because of time constraints, choose only one or two principles and applications from the following list to discuss with the group. In the final minutes of your discussion time, ask the women to complete the "After Your Group Discussion…" box in their workbooks and then share their responses with the group as time permits.

Principles and Applications

Day One: A Bold Bargain

Principle:
- Fleshly desires cannot compare to developing an appetite for the things of God.

Application:
- As you think through the last few days, what rash decisions did you make based on a momentary need or "hunger"—whether for food, control, pleasure, material goods, love, attention, etc.? Were your choices in line with Scripture? How did those decisions affect you? When we allow an immediate human need or desire to overshadow the long-term spiritual consequences, we can make costly mistakes.

Day Two: Older but Not Wiser

Principle:
- God's blessings are not to be devalued or taken for granted.

Application:
- How has God blessed you today? If you were aware of the blessing at the time, how did you thank him? We need to be alert to God's blessings in our lives and continually praise him for his generosity.

Day Three: An Aging Father, a Scheming Mother

Principle:
- Our best sources of wise counsel are God's Word and God's people.

Application:
- As you think about your week, what advice have you taken from another person? Is he or she a child of God? Does that person want the best for you…or for himself or herself? Take into consideration whom you are taking advice from, learn from your mistakes, and next time seek wise, godly counsel.

Day Four: A Hairy Plan

Principle:
- God hates any lie, any deception of others or of ourselves.

Application:
- Review your last few days. What have you thought, said, or done that you wish you could take back? As Christians, our speech and our actions should reflect what is good and right and true so we don't bring reproach on ourselves or on God.

Day Five: Blessings for the Deceiver

Principle:
- We can trust God to honor his promises, just as he honored his promise to bless Abraham, Isaac, and Jacob.

Application:
- Is there something in your past that keeps you from trusting others or even from trusting God fully and completely? Just as God was faithful to honor his promises to these patriarchs, we can trust every promise he has made to us in his Word.

VIDEO

Gather and watch the video as a group.

CLOSING PRAYER/ENCOURAGEMENT FOR THE WEEK

Bring a sense of closure to the class time and point to the next lesson, letting everyone know that in the week ahead they'll be studying certain human behaviors and learning more about God's faithfulness. End with prayer.

LEADER GUIDE

WEEK TWO

Running from God

God Knows All About Prodigal Children

> *Scriptures for the week:*
> Genesis 27:30–28:9

CHECKLIST

☐ Preparation completed
☐ Welcome Warmups copied

WELCOME WARMUP

As the women come in, give them this statement printed on a card: *Think of an example of a prodigal you know. Using discretion, briefly share that person's story.*

OPENING

Begin on time. Welcome the women and open in prayer. As you pray, include elements in the prayer that will bring to mind the past week's lesson as well as point ahead to the principles and applications that will be discussed later in the session. This will help women leave behind any outside distractions and prepare their hearts to focus on the Bible study and the lessons God has for them.

GROUP DISCUSSION

Warmup: Ask people to think of an example of a prodigal they know. Have two or three briefly recount their stories, and then discuss why the testimony of a prodigal may sometimes be more powerful than the testimony of a person who has never turned away from God.

After listening to the women's comments, remind everyone to incorporate what they've learned about prodigals into their discussion of the week's questions by making this point: *You will hear two additional powerful stories of prodigals in today's video.*

Discussion: Have attendees open to their prepared answers for this week's lesson. Cover the most important questions. Because of time constraints, choose only one or two principles and applications from the following list to discuss with the group. In the final minutes of your discussion time, ask the women to complete the "After Your Group Discussion…" box in their workbooks and then share their responses with the group as time permits.

Principles and Applications

Day One: A Matter of Minutes

Principle:
- We must always be aware of our choices and behavior. How we respond to situations can affect the rest of our lives.

Application:
- Have you ever been manipulated into doing something you did not want to do? How did you initially respond to the situation? Looking back, how might you have handled things differently? Even if we have been treated badly, venting our anger only harms us further. A good antidote for anger is remembering God's faithfulness and mercy toward us, even when we deserved *his* anger.

Day Two: Bitter Tears

Principle:
- The consequences of our actions are often unavoidable.

Application:
- What consequences are you living with today because of a selfish action or rash decision in your past? Because God is gracious and full of mercy, we should seriously consider the changes we need to make in our lives—personally, relationally, and especially spiritually—and then take action, rather than continuing to make wrong choices. As children of God, we have the power to start fresh and begin to make godly decisions.

Day Three: Out for Revenge

Principle:
- No matter the situation, it is not our job, but God's, to take revenge.

Application:
- Share an incident where you responded to an unjust situation without seeking godly counsel through prayer or advice from another Christian. Did you try to settle the score? If so, how did you feel afterward? We must release our desire to get even and instead trust God to handle things. If anger and revenge have become habits in our lives, we should look below the surface to determine why.

Day Four: A Family Split

Principle:
- God's promises to his people will be fulfilled no matter how desperate the situation may appear at the moment.

Application:
- Has some aspect of your life wounded you so deeply that you consider yourself unworthy of love? Perhaps you are a victim of abuse, divorce, or alcoholism and still bear the scars. Maybe you have created your own unhappy situation from selfish choices that now affect the people you care about most—a spouse, child, parent, or friend. We may believe we have failed so miserably that God could never forgive or love us again. Yet God has promised his children that he will love them no matter what, that he will forgive them continually, and that he will restore their hearts and cleanse their spirits.

LEADER GUIDE

Day Five: Misguided Steps

Principle:
- Decisions based on resentment, jealousy, or revenge are not honoring to God and will only make matters worse.

Application:
- Make a list of emotions that you have on a daily or weekly basis. Categorize them, noting which emotions are sinful and selfish and which are good and godly. Think of an emotion you expressed recently. Was your response selfish or godly? As we make decisions and plans for our lives, we should measure them against the wisdom of God's Word rather than base them on our changeable emotional states.

VIDEO

Gather and watch the video as a group.

CLOSING PRAYER/ENCOURAGEMENT FOR THE WEEK

Bring a sense of closure to the class time and point to the next lesson, letting everyone know they will see a turn in the story next week as they sense God's presence and begin to understand how much he truly loves his people. End with prayer.

WEEK THREE

A Dream Come True

God's Love Knows No Bounds

Scriptures for the week:
Genesis 28:10-22

CHECKLIST

❏ Preparation completed

❏ Empty chair with "God" sign in place

❏ Welcome Warmups copied

WELCOME WARMUP

As the women come in, give them this statement printed on a card: *As you enter, notice God's chair in the room and acknowledge his presence in some meaningful way.*

OPENING

Begin on time. Welcome the women and open in prayer. As you pray, include elements in the prayer that will bring to mind the past week's lesson as well as point ahead to the principles and applications that will be discussed later in the session. This will help women leave behind any outside distractions and prepare their hearts to focus on the Bible study and the lessons God has for them.

GROUP DISCUSSION

Warmup: You will have already placed a chair in the room and put a sign on it that says "God." At the beginning of the class, explain that they are to act as though God is sitting in that chair, listening to their discussion. Throughout the discussion, continue to remind them of his holy presence as you discuss "God with us."

Notice the mood of the room. Is it quieter than in weeks past? Are nicer words being spoken? Have the women explain any changes from the normal mood of the room. After listening to the women's comments, remind everyone to incorporate what they've learned about God's holy presence into their discussion of the week's questions by making this point: *Although God's chair is at the front of the room, he can hear your conversations in your small group, too, and can discern the thoughts and intentions of your heart.*

Discussion: Have attendees open to their prepared answers for this week's lesson. Cover the most important questions. Because of time constraints, choose only one or two principles and applications from the following list to discuss with the group. In the final minutes of your discussion time, ask the women to complete the "After Your Group Discussion…" box in their workbooks and then share their responses with the group as time permits.

Principles and Applications

Day One: Divine Communication

Principle:
- God comes to help those who are unworthy of his help.

Application:
- What have you done in your life that you don't think God will ever overlook? Is it a damaging lie, an affair, abusive behavior, or an illegal action? God takes us as we are. Jacob did not "deserve" God's help, and yet God extended it. In the same way, although we are undeserving of God's attention, God loves us "as is." Indeed, "God is our refuge and strength, an ever-present help in trouble" (Psalm 46:1).

Day Two: God's Promise and Presence

Principle:
- When God speaks, it is with authority, and we know that he has spoken.

Application:
- Has there been an instance in your life when you knew God "spoke" to you? Maybe it was during your prayer time, or maybe he communicated to you through a friend, spouse, or parent. Share your experience with the group. If you cannot give an example of this in your life, perhaps it's a matter of perception. You may have credited someone or something else for a word of wisdom that came from on high. God desires to communicate with each of us, and he does this through his Word, through prayer, and through fellowship with other believers. Become aware of the truth that God wants to have a relationship with you, and begin to listen for the ways he is speaking to you.

Day Three: Sacred Sites

Principle:
- The "fear of the Lord"—giving him the reverence, respect, and honor due him—brings life.

Application:
- What words would you use to describe your view of God? How has your perception of him changed over the years? We are not to be afraid of God, seeing him as angry and judgmental and watching to catch us in a mistake so he can punish us. Instead, we are to be in awe of a perfectly holy God who loves his highly imperfect people.

Day Four: More Than a Name Change

Principle:
- The most important decision we can ever make is to commit to the Lord that he will be our God.

Application:
- Have you committed your life to the Lord? If so, will you share that publicly during this time of discussion? That commitment changes everything in our lives—what we say, what we do, how we spend our time, how we treat other people, and ultimately where we will spend eternity.

Day Five: Jacob's Promises and Offerings

Principle:
- God gives to us so that we can give back to him. Our attitude should be right so that we give freely and cheerfully.

Application:
- What gift has God given you that you might use to bless others? Maybe it's a financial gift, a musical talent, the ability to teach, or simply the desire to serve. Periodically look at the gifts and blessings God has given you, and determine if you're purposefully giving back your time, money, and talents to God.

VIDEO

Gather and watch the video as a group.

CLOSING PRAYER/ENCOURAGEMENT FOR THE WEEK

Bring a sense of closure to the class time and point to the next lesson, explaining that next week they will consider the difference between our "inside" selves and our "outside" selves and will discuss what commitment means. End with prayer.

LEADER GUIDE

WEEK FOUR

Blinded by Love

*Man Looks at the Outward Appearance;
God Looks at the Heart*

CHECKLIST

❑ Preparation completed

❑ Welcome Warmups copied

Scriptures for the week:
Genesis 29:1-20

WELCOME WARMUP

As the women come in, give them this statement printed on a card: *Silently choose someone in the room and quickly write down the first three things you notice about that person. Next, write down three important qualities any person should have.*

OPENING

Begin on time. Welcome the women and open in prayer. As you pray, include elements in the prayer that will bring to mind the past week's lesson as well as point ahead to the principles and applications that will be discussed later in the session. This will help women leave behind any outside distractions and prepare their hearts to focus on the Bible study and the lessons God has for them.

GROUP DISCUSSION

Warmup: Make sure everyone had time to jot down quickly the first three things they *noticed* about the person they selected and what they consider to be the three most important *qualities* of a person. If a chalkboard or whiteboard is available, make a list of their top choice in both categories. If no board is available, simply have the women share their lists.

After listening to the women's comments, remind everyone to incorporate what they've learned about inward and outward attributes into their discussion of the week's questions by making this point: *Although we focus on our external qualities, God looks at our internal qualities. Think about how you can change your viewpoint to be more like God's.*

Discussion: Have attendees open to their prepared answers for this week's lesson. Cover the most important questions. Because of time constraints, choose only one or two principles and applications from the following list to discuss with the group. In the final minutes of your discussion time, ask the women to complete the "After Your Group Discussion…" box in their workbooks and then share their responses with the group as time permits.

Principles and Applications

Day One: Journey's End

Principle:
- When we become a child of God, our character changes to become more like him, but the transformation is a lifetime process.

Application:
- What characteristics about yourself do you see changing as you draw closer to God? Some people may notice drastic changes while others detect more subtle shifts in attitude and behavior, yet God sees them all, big and small.

Day Two: Jacob Meets His Love

Principle:
- God will give us strength and purpose when we are committed to him.

Application:
- What is happening in your life right now that requires God's strength to endure? If you will commit your situation to him, he will give you the strength you need.

Day Three: Jacob Meets His Match

Principle:
- We should be quick to listen and slow to speak, choosing our words carefully.

Application:
- What decision have you made this week without considering all the aspects involved? What could be the consequences? Most of us are slow to listen and quick to speak! If we would simply follow God's order—quick to listen, slow to speak—we might avoid future heartache.

Day Four: Beauty Seen and Unseen

Principle:
- The outward beauty of others may steer us in the wrong direction.

Application:
- When you walk into a roomful of strangers, are you drawn to people who look successful or say the right things in a meeting or have material possessions you would like to own? Maybe you reach out to others who look like you, or perhaps you seek friendships with women who are quite the opposite of you. As we learn to care more about our appearance to God and less about our appearance to others, we will become more "beautiful" on the inside, and our outward appearance will be transformed as well. In the same manner, we should accept people the way God created them to be and not make shallow judgments based on appearance.

Day Five: The Price of Love

Principle:
- Once you make a commitment, do everything possible to fulfill your obligation.

Application:
- Think of a commitment you have made recently—a work project, a promise to a child, or an agreement to pray for a friend. Have you kept your commitment? It's important to act with integrity. When you vow to do something, big or small, think of it as a commitment to God himself and keep your commitment to the end.

VIDEO

Gather and watch the video as a group.

CLOSING PRAYER/ENCOURAGEMENT FOR THE WEEK

Bring a sense of closure to the class time and point to the next lesson, telling everyone to expect the unexpected in next week's portion of the biblical story as we watch God's discipline at work in Jacob's life and in ours. End with prayer.

Loved by God

WEEK FIVE

A Deceiver Deceived

God Disciplines the Ones He Loves

Scriptures for the week:
Genesis 29:21-29

CHECKLIST

❏ Preparation completed
❏ Welcome Warmups copied

WELCOME WARMUP

As the women come in, give them this statement printed on a card: *What rules would you recommend for disciplining an adult in a work situation who has violated a company policy?*

OPENING

Begin on time. Welcome the women and open in prayer. As you pray, include elements in the prayer that will bring to mind the past week's lesson as well as point ahead to the principles and applications that will be discussed later in the session. This will help women leave behind any outside distractions and prepare their hearts to focus on the Bible study and the lessons God has for them.

GROUP DISCUSSION

Warmup: Using a chalkboard, whiteboard, poster board, or large tablet, ask the class to give you their "rules" for disciplining adults in a work situation. Then compare that list to the one God might generate if he were explaining why he disciplines us. Follow up with a discussion of the nature and value of God's discipline.

After writing both kinds of discipline on the board—human and divine—encourage your women to think about this exercise as they go into their discussion time by emphasizing this point: *Consider why it is important to know and understand God's discipline.*

Discussion: Have attendees open to their prepared answers for this week's lesson. Cover the most important questions. Because of time constraints, choose only one or two principles and applications from the following list to discuss with the group. In the final minutes of your discussion time, ask the women to complete the "After Your Group Discussion…" box in their workbooks and then share their responses with the group as time permits.

Principles and Applications

Day One: A Big Switch

Principle:
- Following God doesn't insulate a person from mistreatment and sorrow.

Application:
- Have you suffered through a recent ordeal that caught you by surprise, even though you were honestly doing everything right? When we find ourselves in difficult circumstances, the question to ask is not "Where is God in this?" or "Why did God let this happen?" but "How can God use me in this situation for a good purpose?"

Days Two: Vixen or Victim?

Principle:
- We are responsible to God for our actions.

Application:
- Think of an unfortunate incident in your life that never should have happened. Were you the instigator or the victim? Is there anything you can do now to make it right? Perhaps you need to pray for forgiveness for your actions or forgiveness for your bitterness resulting from the situation. Nothing is accomplished by blaming others.

Day Three: Just Deserts?

Principle:
- As sinners, we deserve to die—"For the wages of sin is death." But God saves us through his gift of grace—"the gift of God is eternal life in Christ Jesus our Lord" (Romans 6:23).

Application:
- Do you find yourself pointing out the sins of others rather than recognizing your own sins? Instead of expending our energy ensuring that others get what they "deserve," we should be grateful for the great mercy we have received from God and extend that mercy to others.

Day Four: A Rude Awakening

Principle:
- Although our anger may be directed toward another person, our underlying anger is often aimed at God.

Application:
- Recall an event in your life that you thought was unfair. What emotional baggage do you still bear from that situation, and why are you still carrying it? What can you do to begin to recover from this situation—to heal, to forgive, and to move on? Whether we feel angry, bitter, sad, or lonely, those emotions can interfere with our relationship with God if we find ourselves blaming him for our disappointment. To strengthen our relationship with God, we must deal with our emotions and allow him to heal us.

Day Five: A Second Wife

Principle:
- We reap what we sow. "The one who sows to please his sinful nature, from that nature will reap destruction" (Galatians 6:8).

Application:
- Are there areas in your thought life that have begun to spiral out of control? Although no one can see our thoughts, they *can* see the results since our thoughts control our words and actions. It's easy to see that Jacob reaped the heartache he sowed. It's harder to face those results in our own lives. We must take these sins as seriously as God does, realizing the great consequences they have on others and on our spiritual lives.

VIDEO

Gather and watch the video as a group.

CLOSING PRAYER/ENCOURAGEMENT FOR THE WEEK

Bring a sense of closure to the class time and point to the next lesson, reminding the group that they have only one week left in this Bible study, the most important week of all, which demonstrates the power of God's love and how it can change our hearts and lives for eternity. Encourage them not to miss next week—we've saved the best for last! Then end with prayer.

LEADER GUIDE

WEEK SIX

A Heart for God

God's Love Is Powerful Enough to Change Our Hearts

CHECKLIST

❏ Preparation completed
❏ Welcome Warmups copied

WELCOME WARMUP

As the women come in, give them this statement printed on a card: *Write out your own words of praise to God, thanking him for something good that has happened to you through this study. If you have a favorite psalm, share that as well.*

OPENING

Begin on time. Welcome the women and open in prayer. As you pray, include elements in the prayer that will bring to mind the past week's lesson as well as point ahead to the principles and applications that will be discussed later in the session. This will help women leave behind any outside distractions and prepare their hearts to focus on the Bible study and the lessons God has for them.

GROUP DISCUSSION

Warmup: Taking your cue from Leah, begin with an extended time of praise to God. Ask several class members to share their written praises or read a few verses from their favorite psalm. Sing a praise song together, or ask several people to add their brief thoughts to an opening prayer of praise.

After your time of worship, remind everyone to incorporate what they've learned about praising God into their discussion of the week's questions by making this point: *There were three goals for this Bible study. Praise God for any and all of these changes he has made in your life.*

1. Have you come to realize how much God loves you?
2. Have you learned to trust his promises…and his timing?
3. Have you experienced God's blessings…and redefined "blessing"?

Discussion: Have attendees open to their prepared answers for this week's lesson. Cover the most important questions. Because of time constraints, choose only one or two principles and applications from the following list to discuss with the group. In the final minutes of your discussion time, ask the women to complete the "After Your Group Discussion…" box in their workbooks and then share their responses with the group as time permits.

> *Scriptures for the week:*
> Genesis 29:30-35

Principles and Applications

Day One: Room for Two?

Principle:
- What man considers "manipulation," God may call "discipline," using the situation to mold us into the image of his Son.

Application:
- Is there a situation in your life—a close relationship, a job, a friendship—that's hard for you to handle and often doesn't seem fair? What have you learned from that situation? When we go through hardships, God will use them for our ultimate good and for the purpose of drawing us closer to him.

Day Two: Precious in God's Sight

Principle:
- God sees us, values us, loves us, and comforts us.

Application:
- Have you been through a difficult trial where you felt completely alone, abandoned, even unloved? Perhaps the death of a parent, the loss of a child, or a painful divorce? What a comfort to know we are *not* alone. God sees our circumstances and responds in love.

Day Three: Blessings for the Humble

Principle:
- "God opposes the proud but gives grace to the humble" (James 4:6) and meets their deepest needs.

Application:
- When does God reveal himself most to you—in prosperity or adversity? In easy circumstances or difficult ones? As we see God at work in our lives, we can begin relinquishing our will to God's, giving him the glory for whatever happens rather than taking credit ourselves.

Day Four: The One Who Always Hears

Principle:
- God blesses us in order to demonstrate his character.

Application:
- In what ways have you been blessed this week—whether a visible blessing or the silent blessing of being still and knowing that he is God? Did you deserve the blessings you received? What did you learn about God during those times of blessing? We don't have to earn God's love or do anything to receive his blessing.

Day Five: Praise the Lord

Principle:
- God deserves our full and complete praise.

Application:
- How has your day been? Your week? Can you praise God for every hour, even if some of them didn't go as you had hoped? As we grow in our knowledge of God—who he is and what he has done for us—our hearts fill with love and our lips with gratitude and praise.

VIDEO

Gather and watch the video as a group.

CLOSING PRAYER/ENCOURAGEMENT FOR THE WEEK

Bring a sense of closure to the class time and to this study. Thank the women for participating faithfully each week, and encourage them to continue to think about what they have learned and to stay in God's Word daily. Assure them that they truly are "loved by God"…and so, dear leader, are you! Then end with prayer.

More Exciting Video Seminars from Sampson Resources!

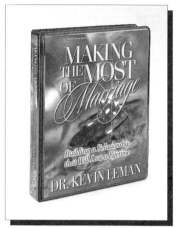

Making the Most of Marriage
*Building a Relationship
that Will Last a Lifetime*
DR. KEVIN LEMAN

Single Parenting That Works!
*Raising Well-Balanced Children
in an Off-Balanced World*
DR. KEVIN LEMAN

**Making Children Mind
Without Losing Yours**
*How to Bring Out the Best in Kids
By Doing What is Best for Them*
DR. KEVIN LEMAN

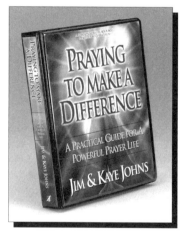

Praying to Make A Difference
*A Practical Guide for
A Powerful Prayer Life*
JIM & KAYE JOHNS

*To learn more about our ministry resources
that are in thousands of churches, visit:*

www.sampsonresources.com